FASHION SKETCHBOOK

Figure & Flat Template

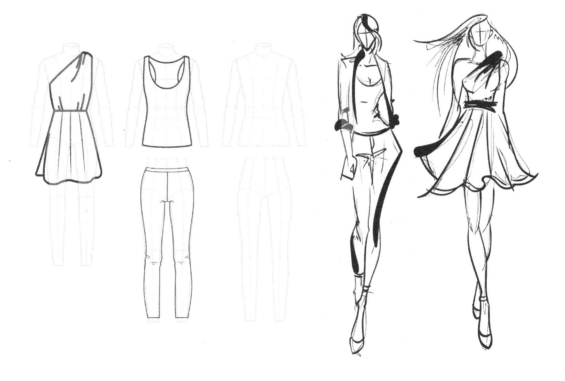

_____

_____

Shirts

Dress

Skirts

Pants

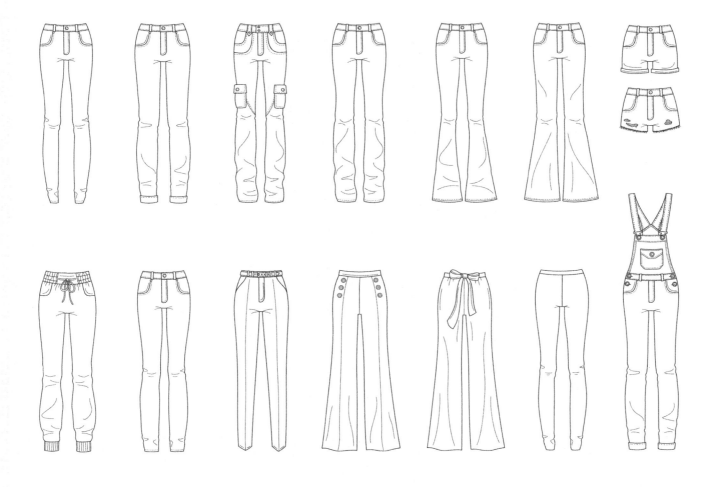

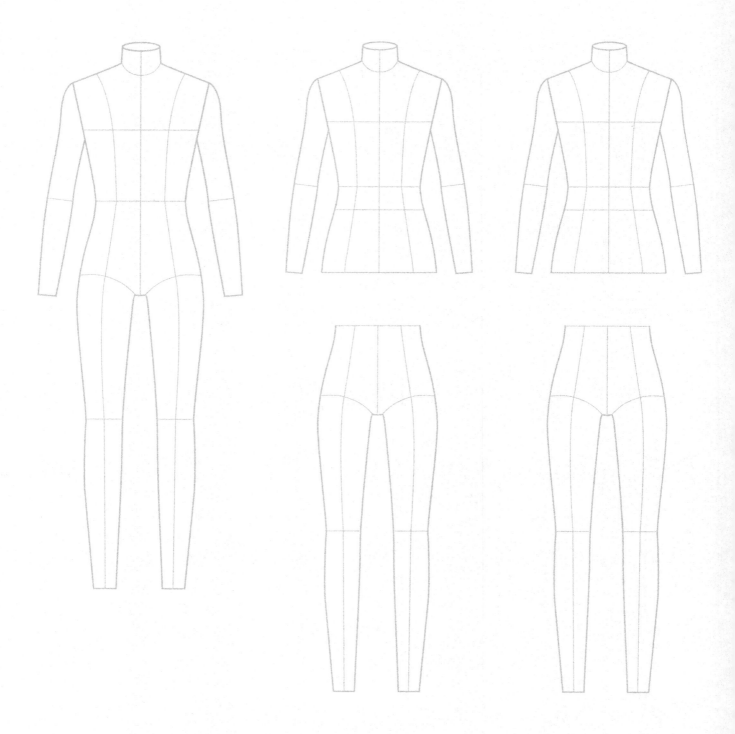

Note

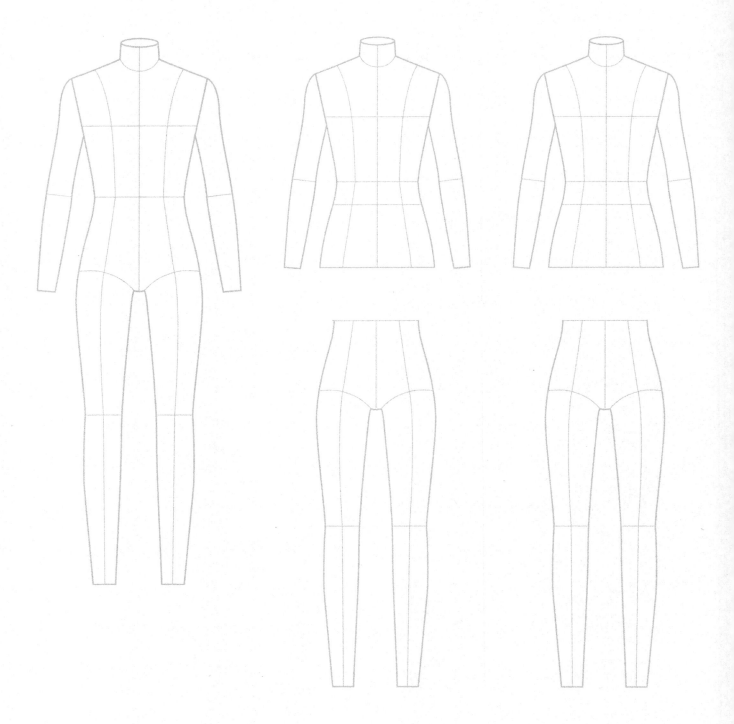

Note

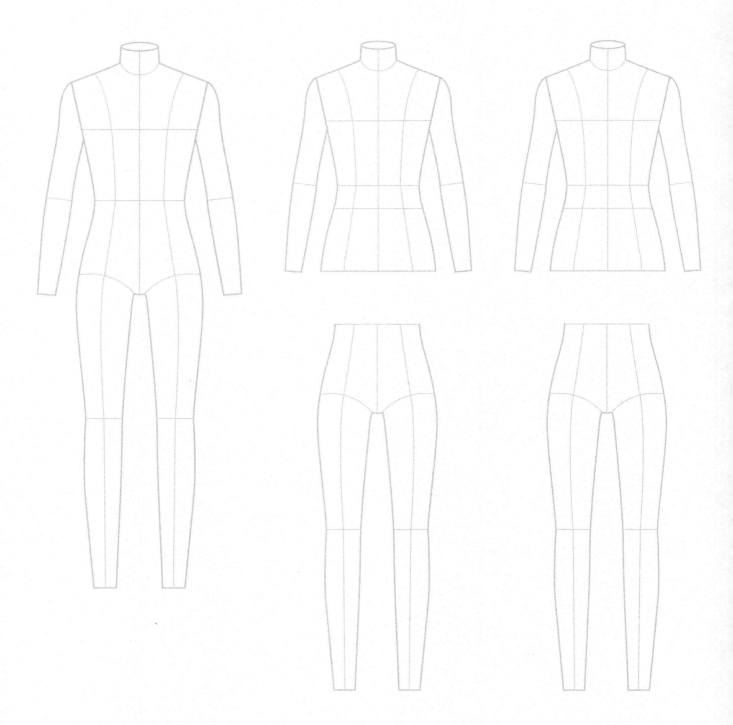

Note

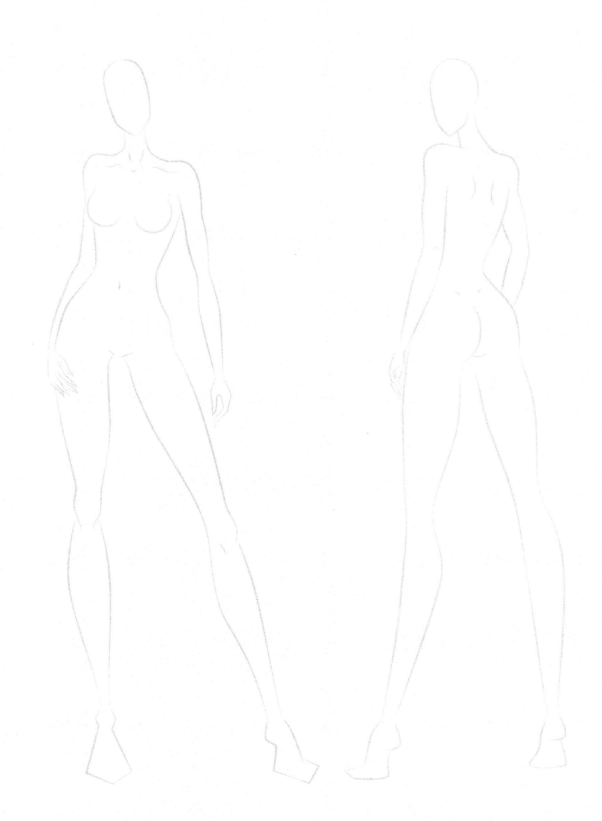

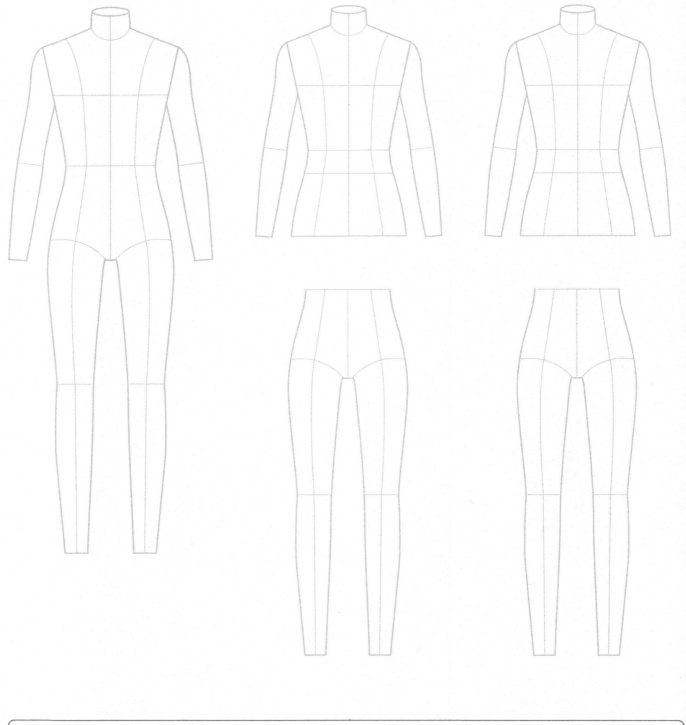

Note

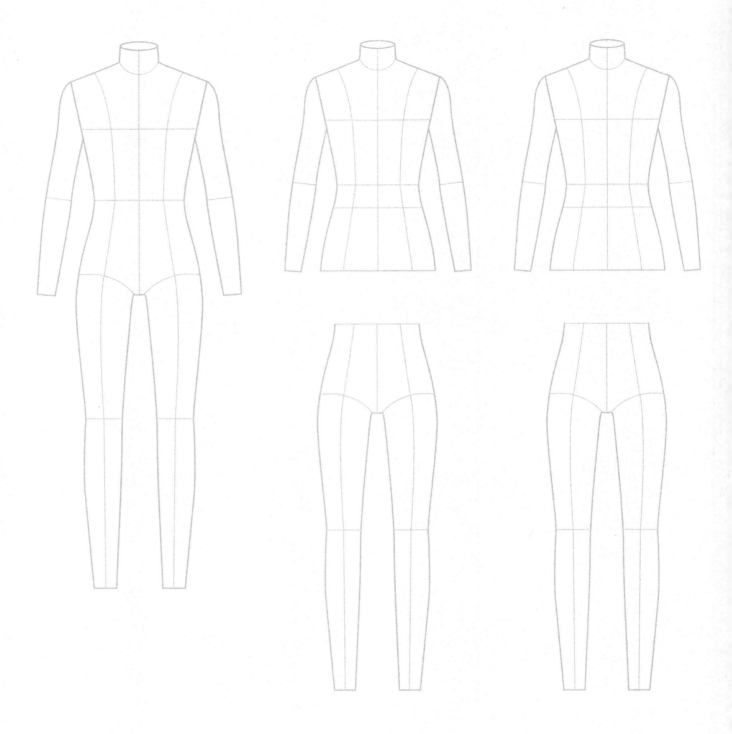

Note

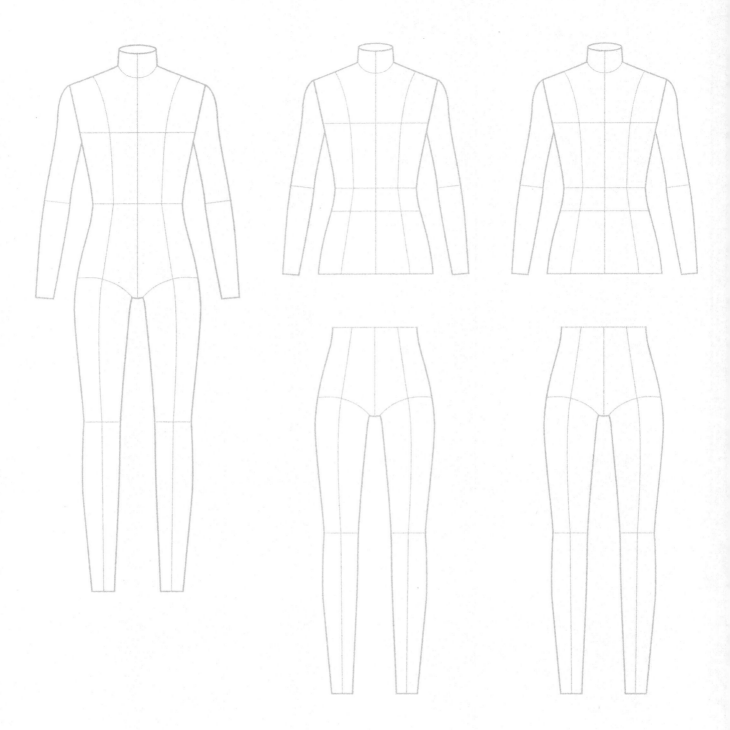

Note

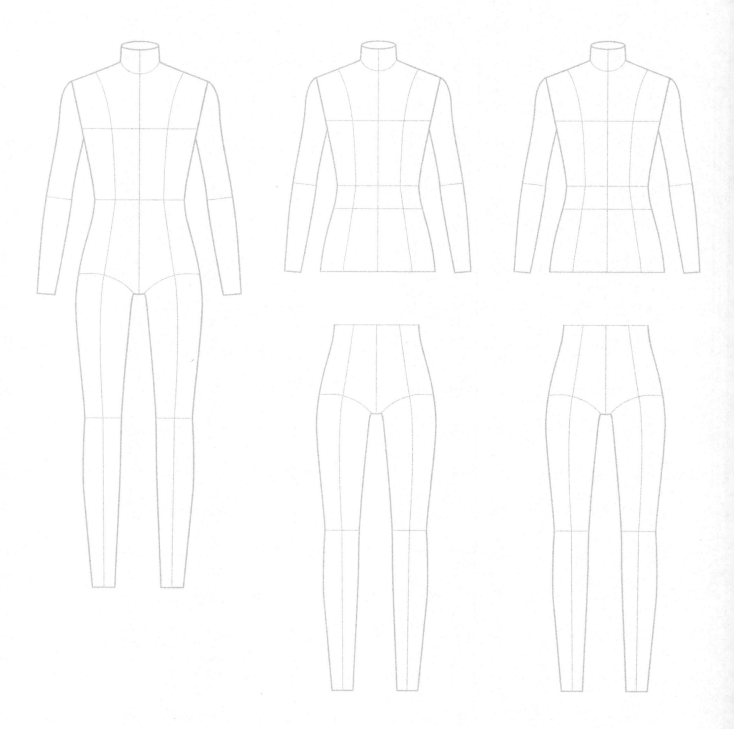

Note

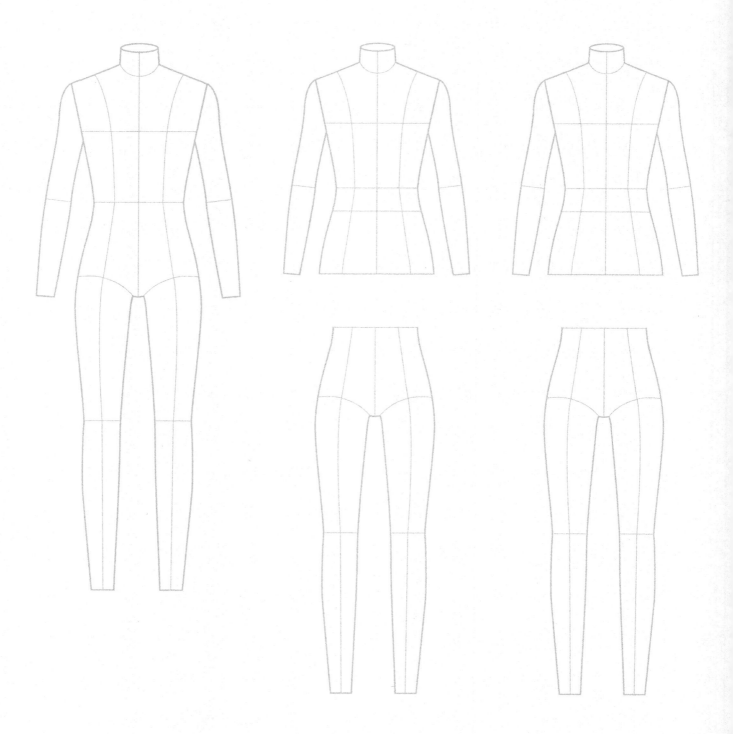

Note

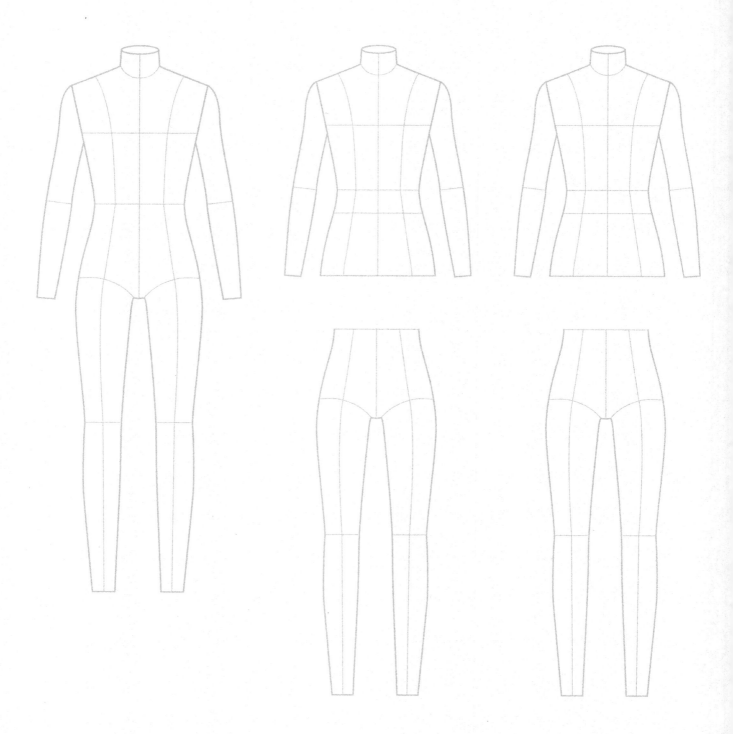

Note

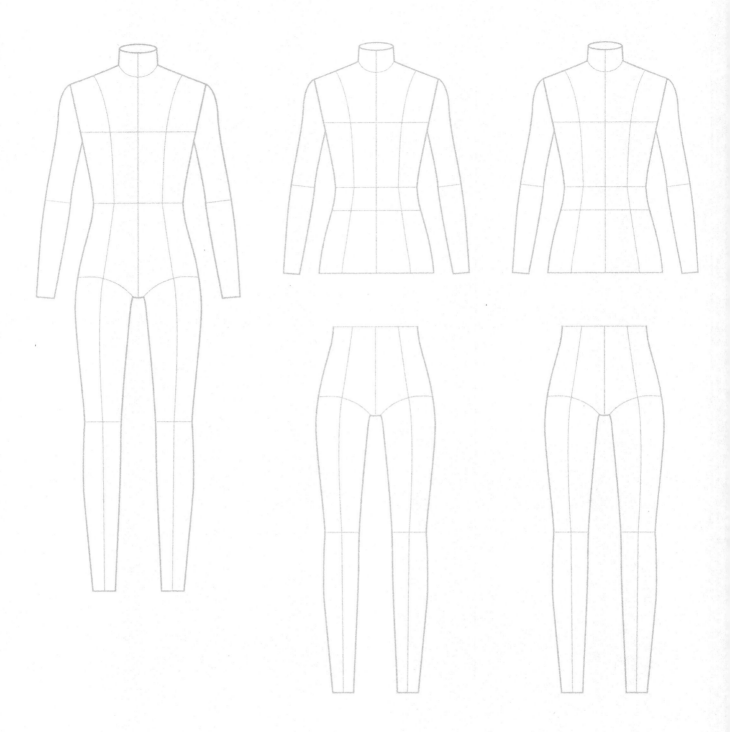

Note

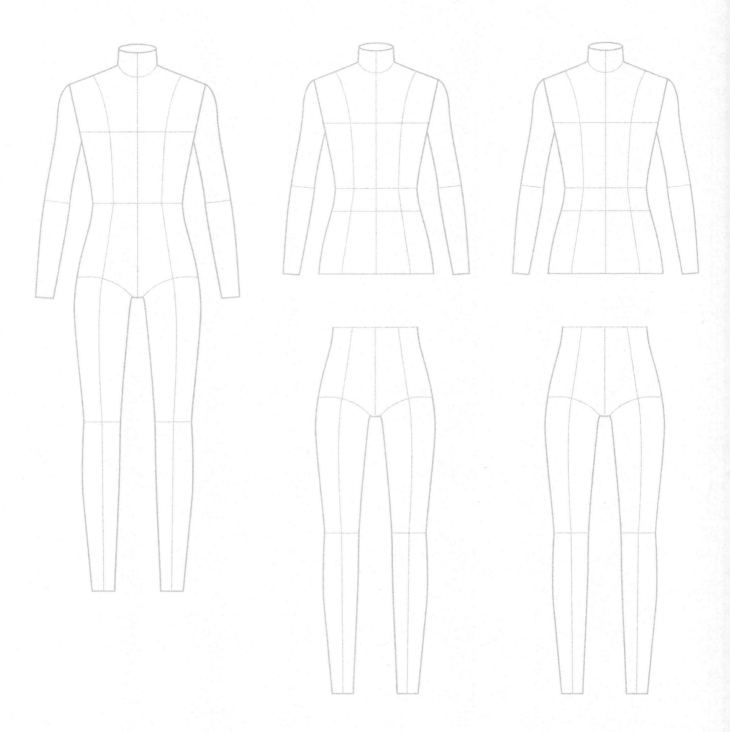

Note

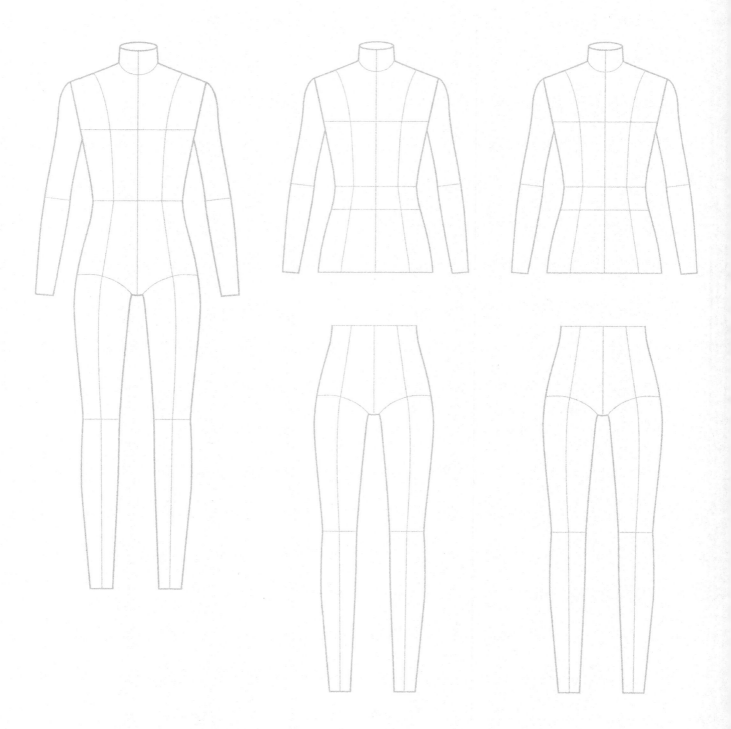

Note

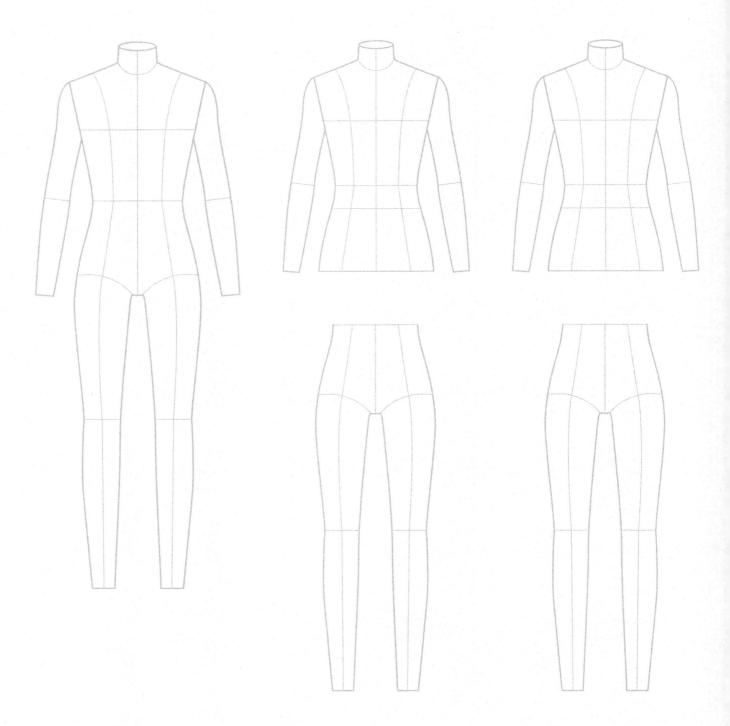

Note

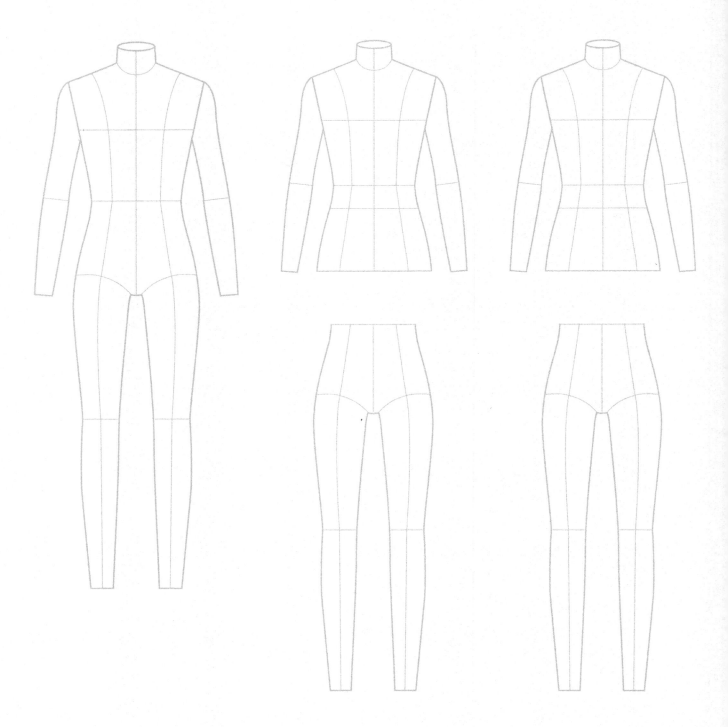

Note

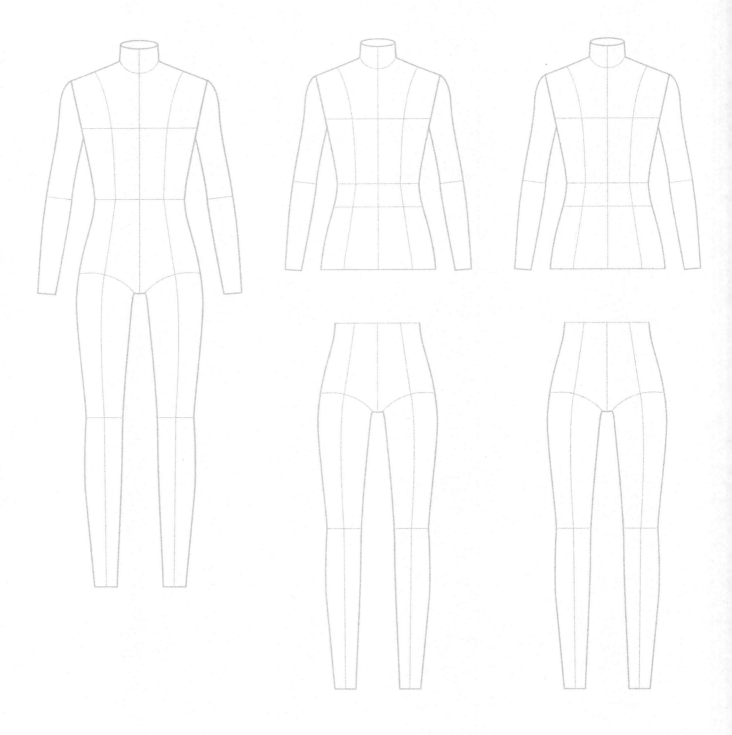

Note

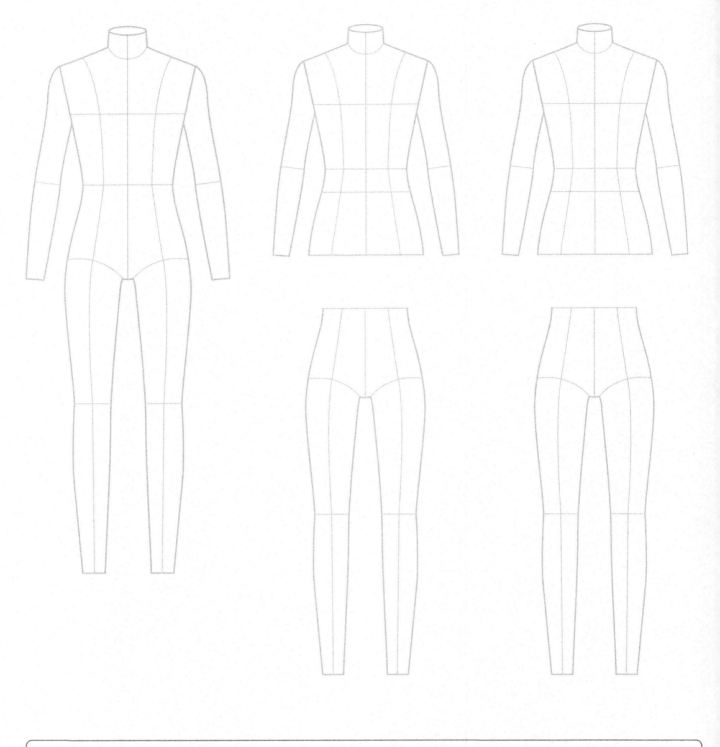

Note

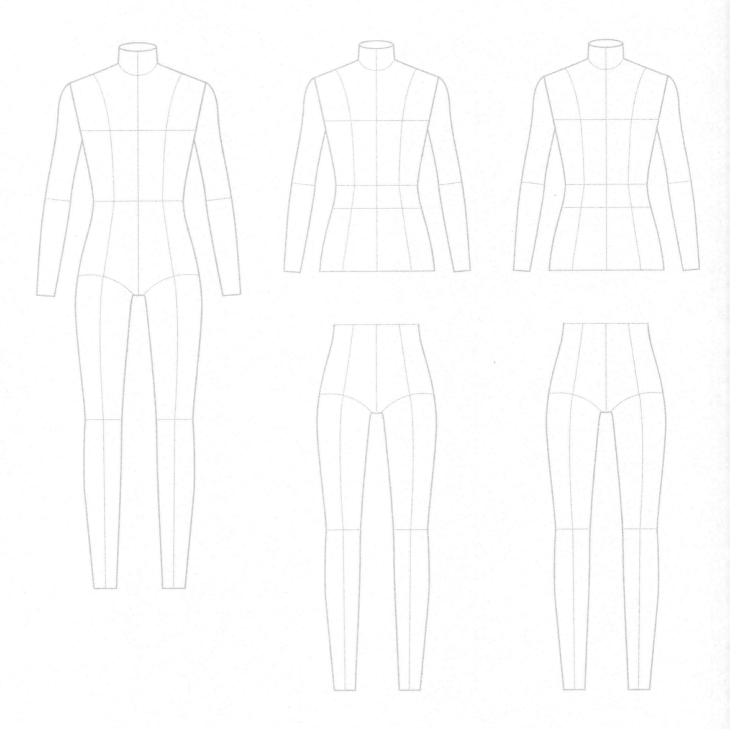

Note

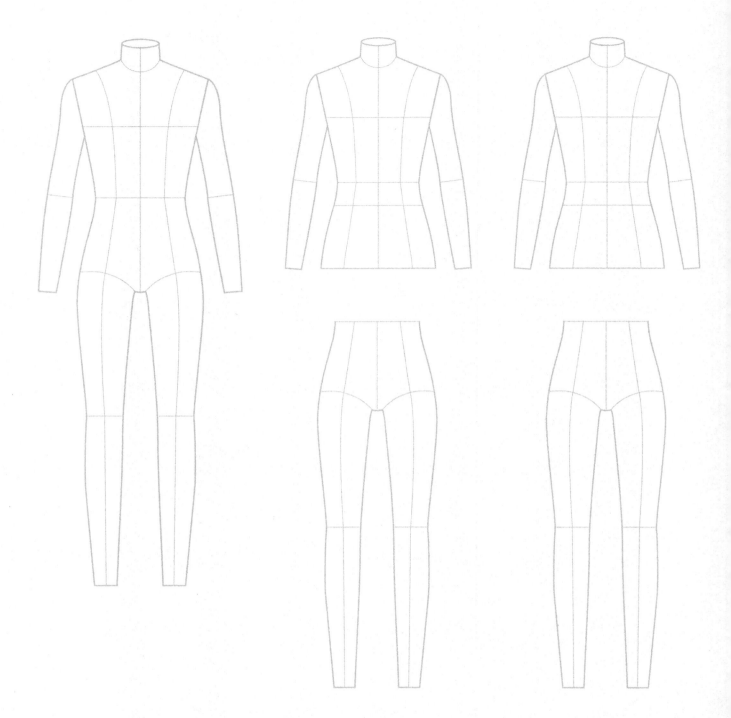

Note

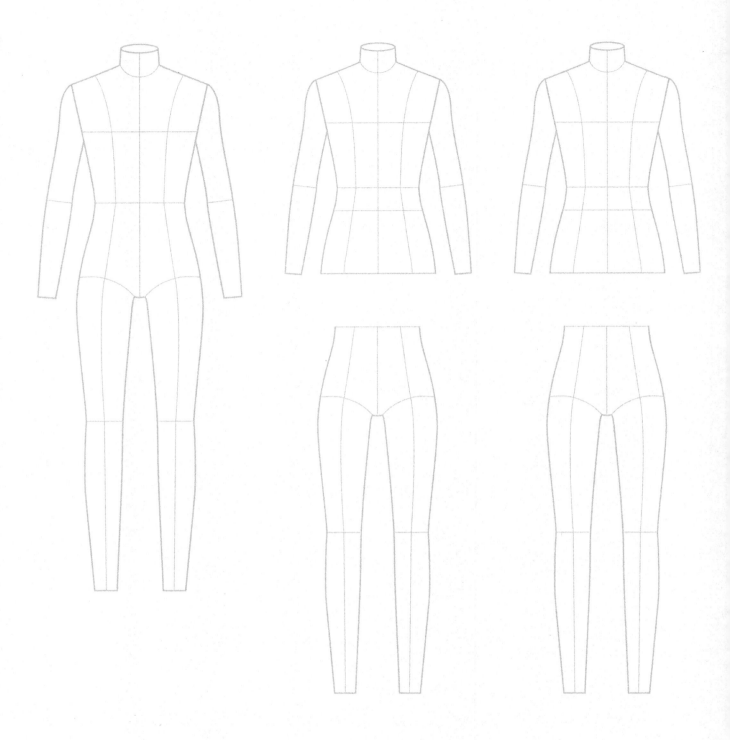

Note

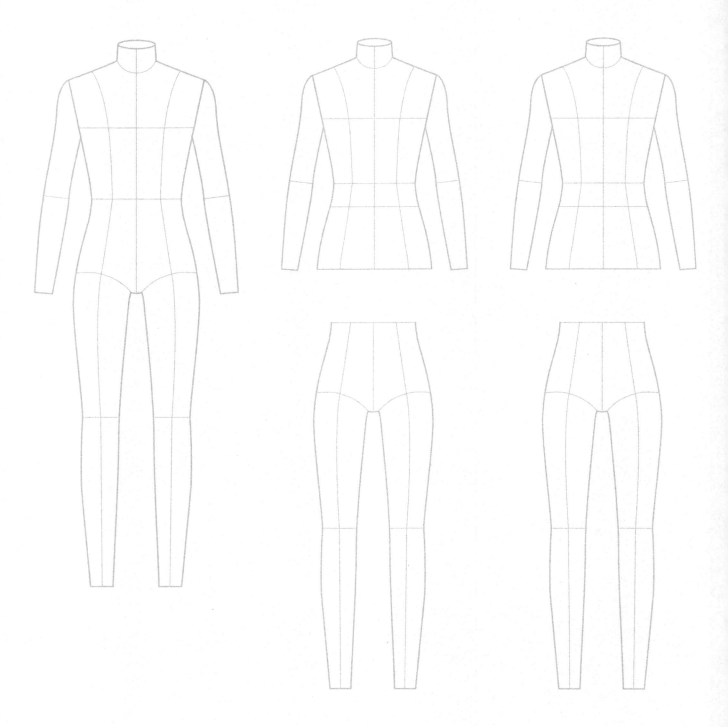

Note

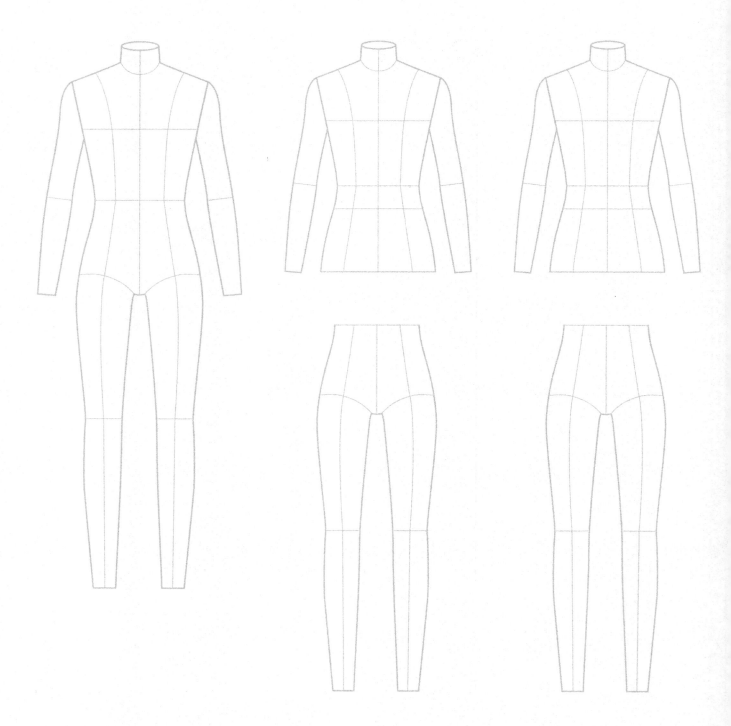

Note

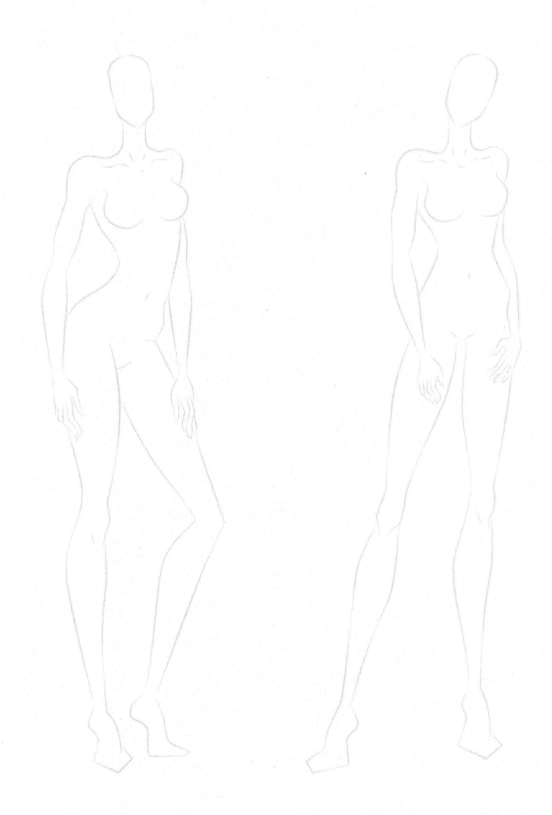

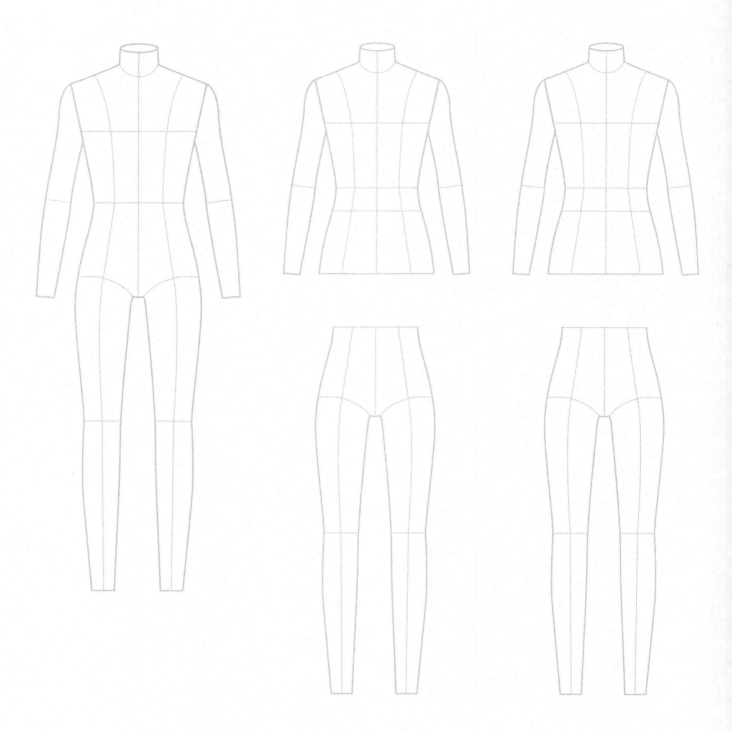

Note

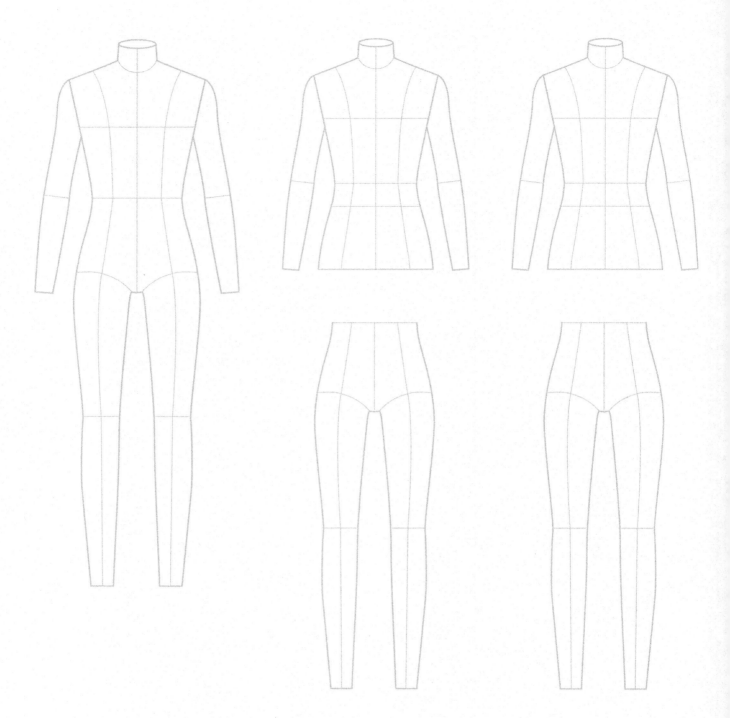

Note

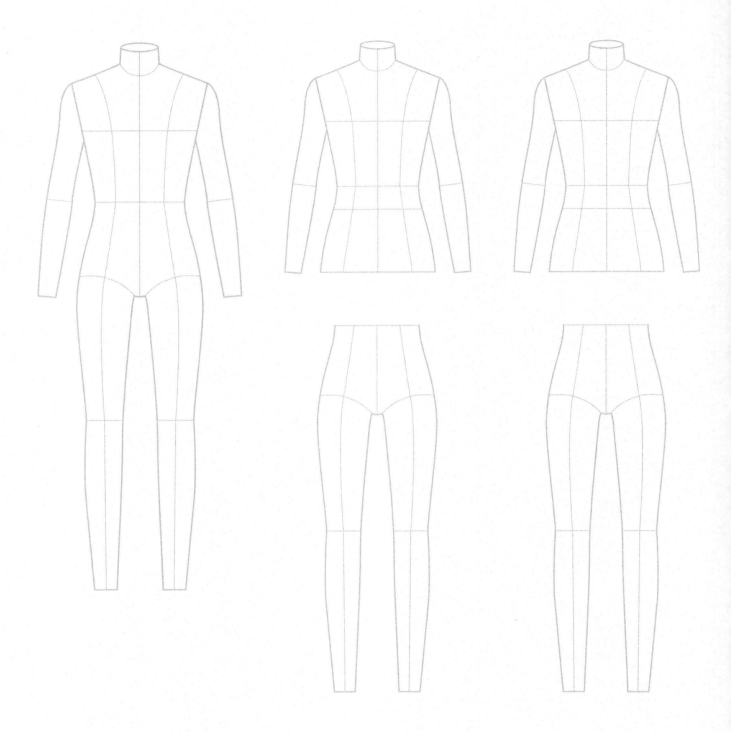

Note

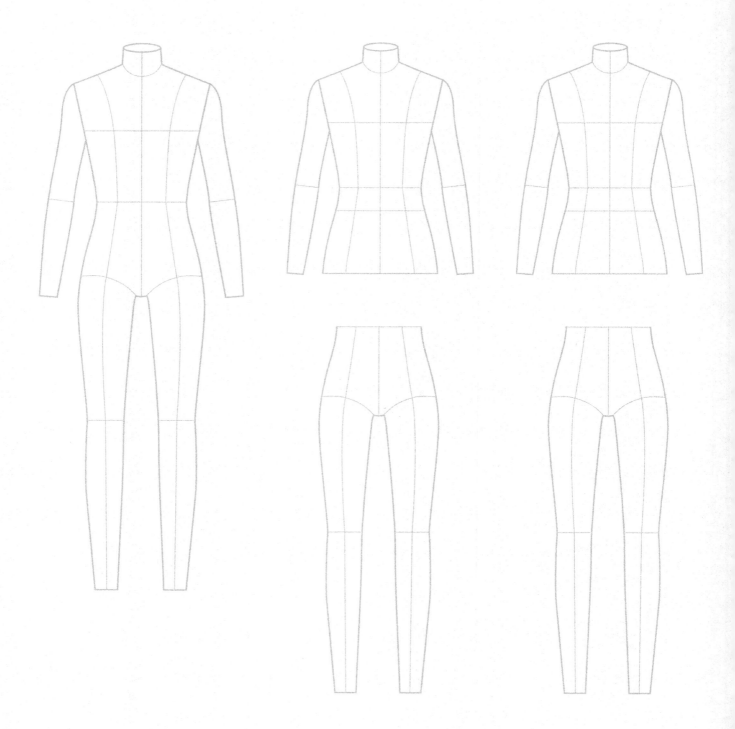

Note

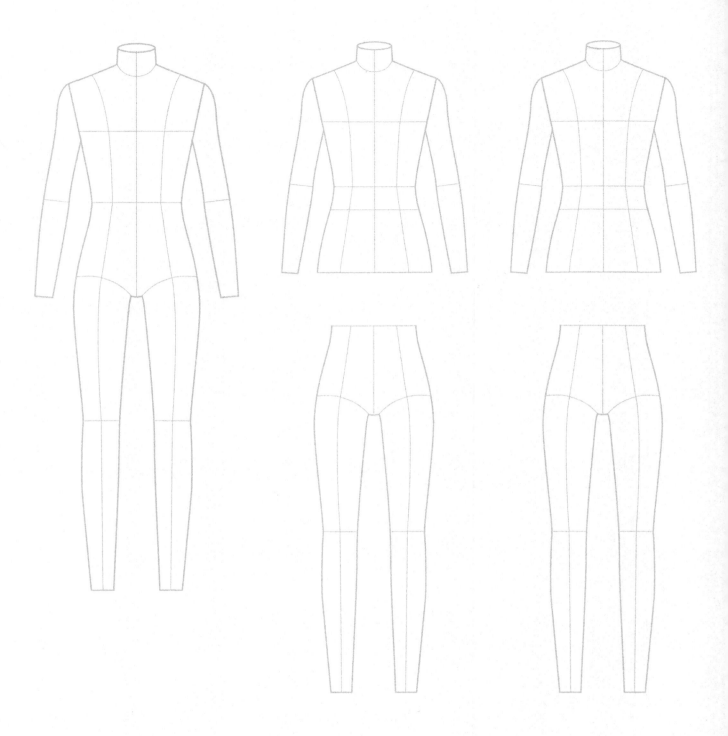

Note

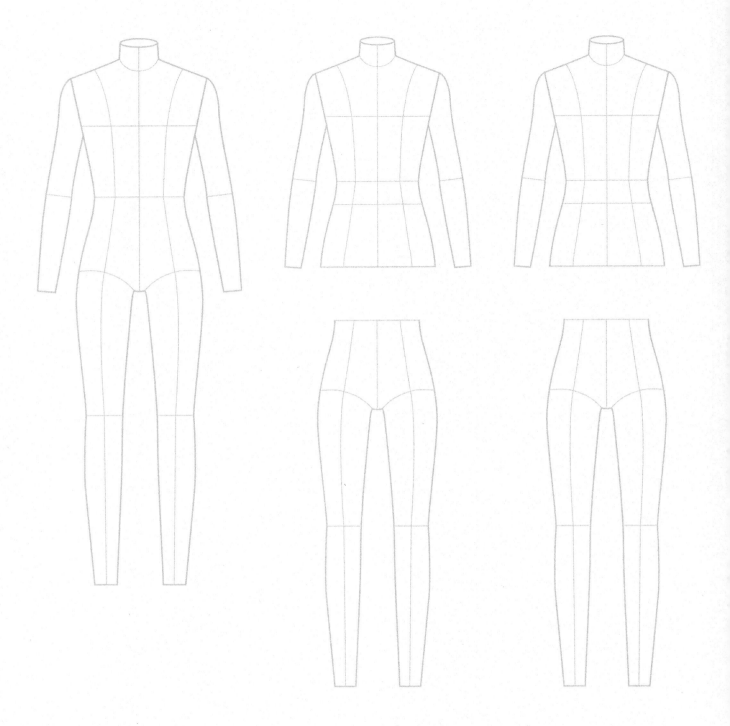

Note

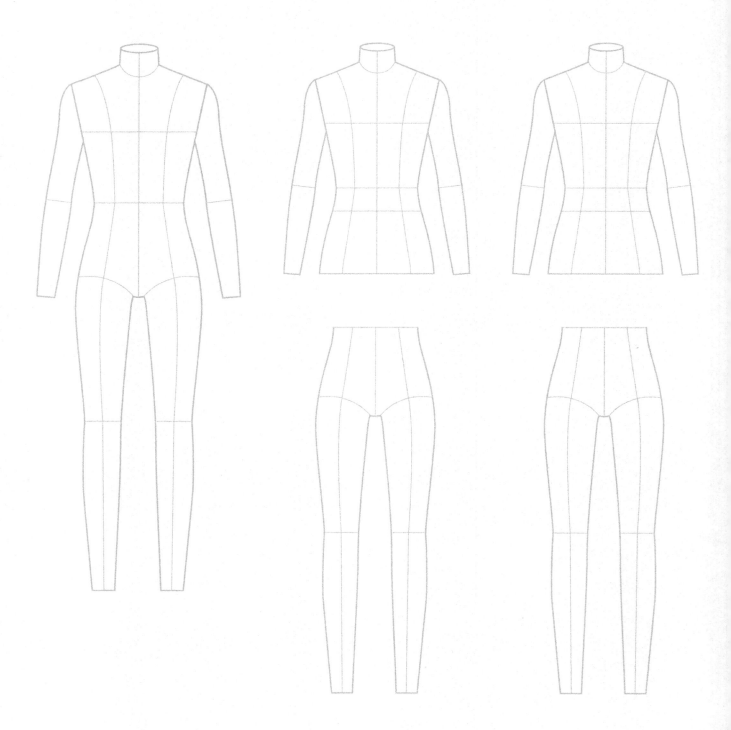

Note

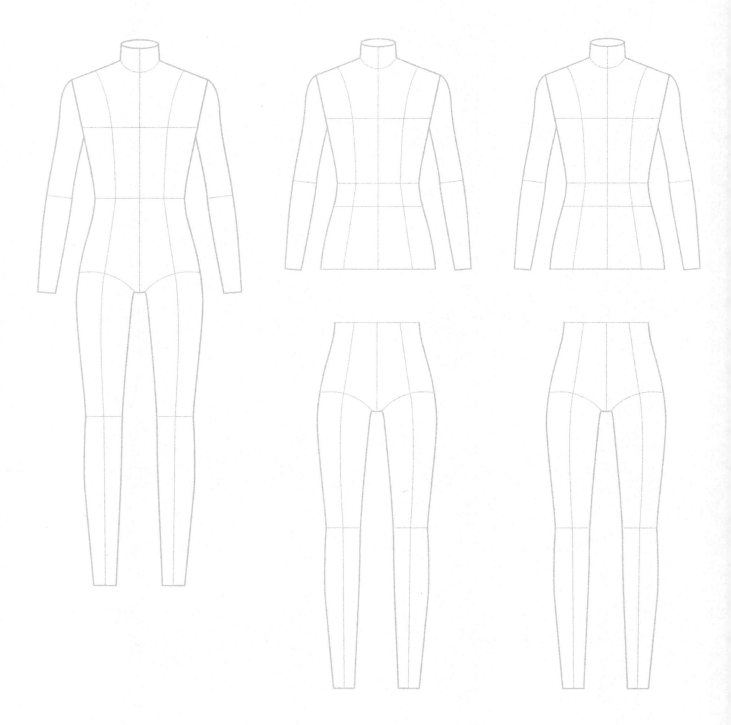

Note

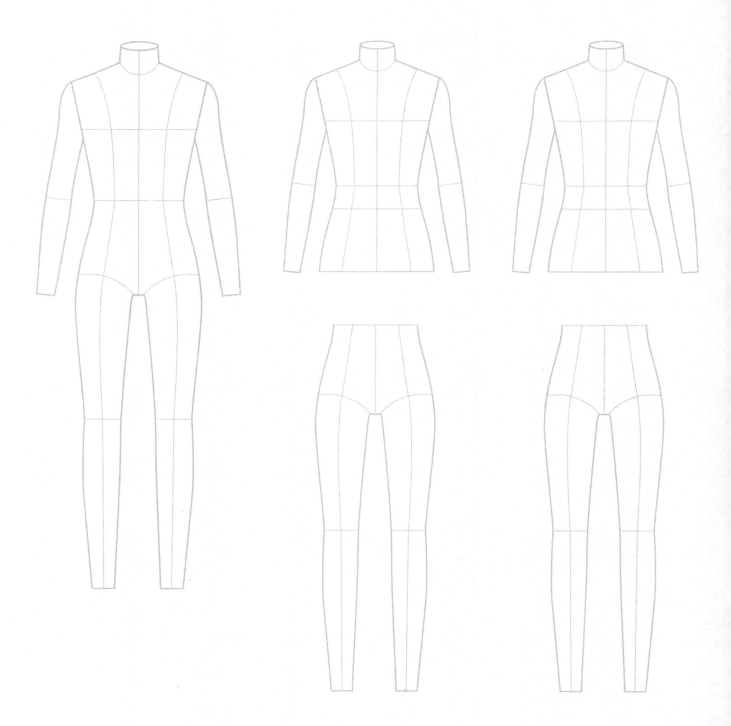

Note

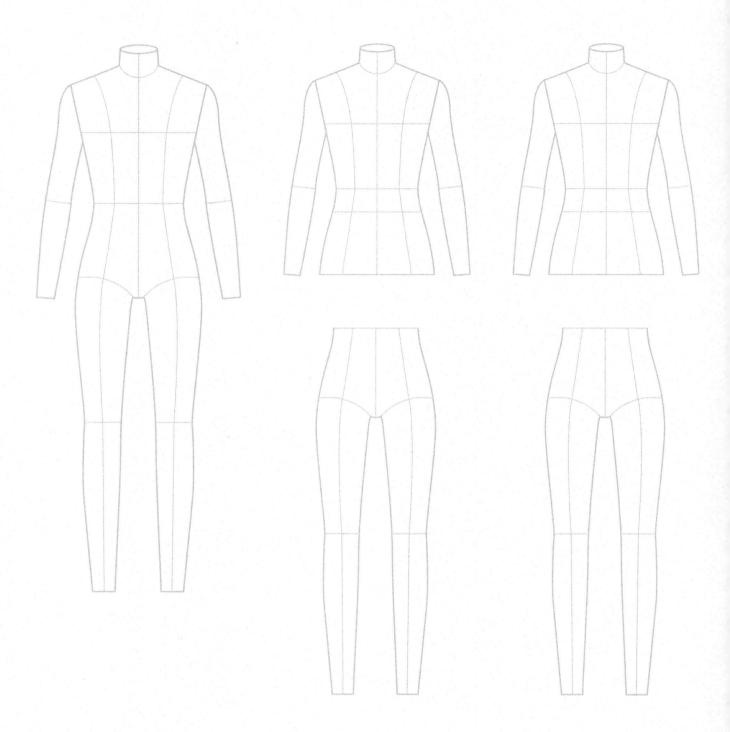

Note

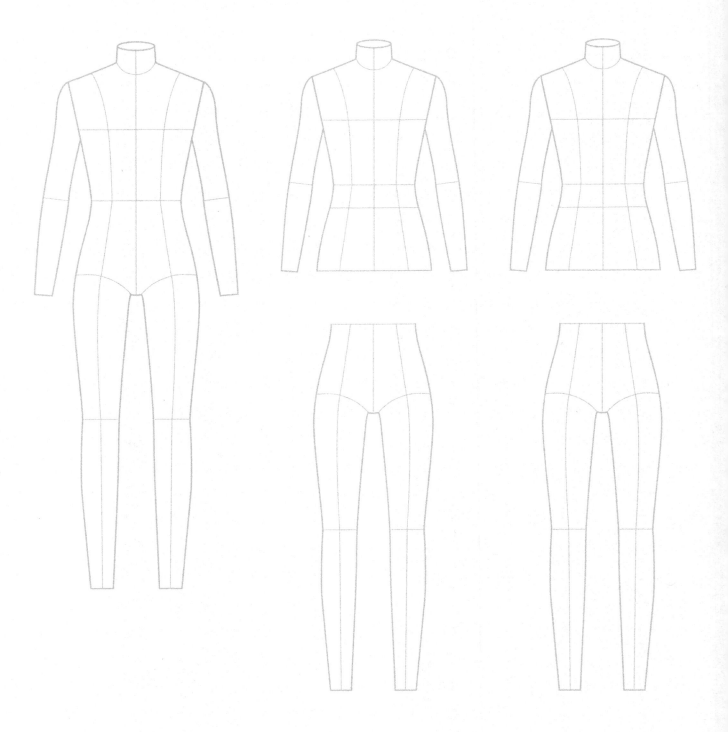

Note

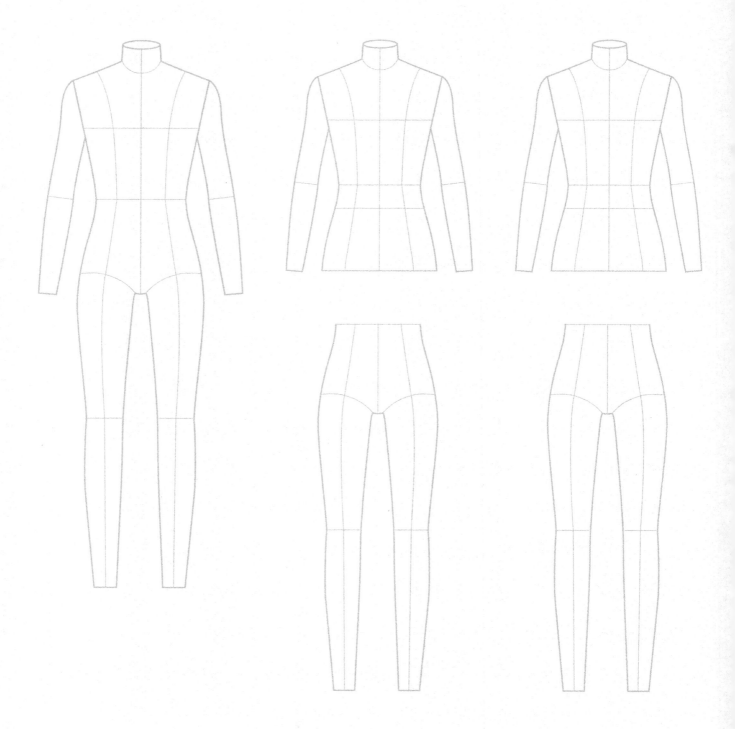

Note

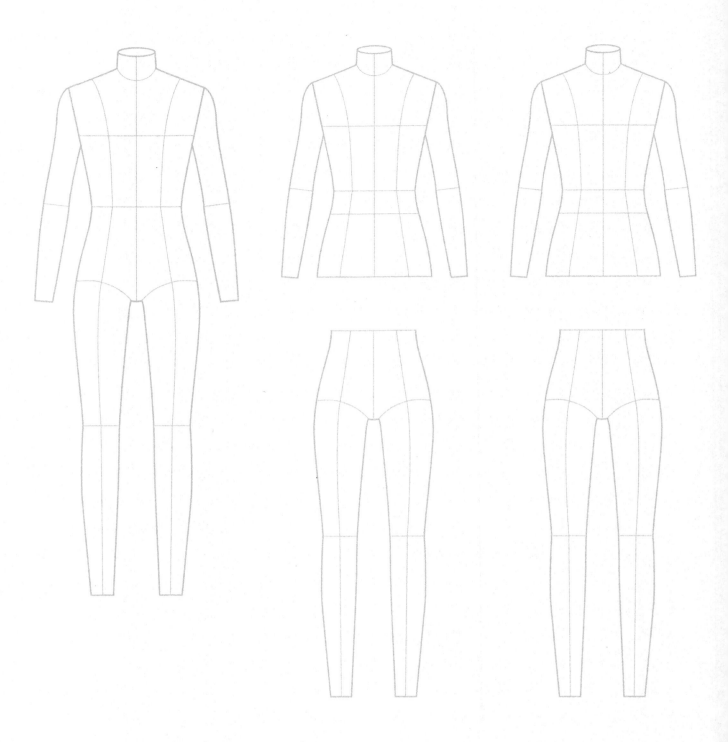

Note

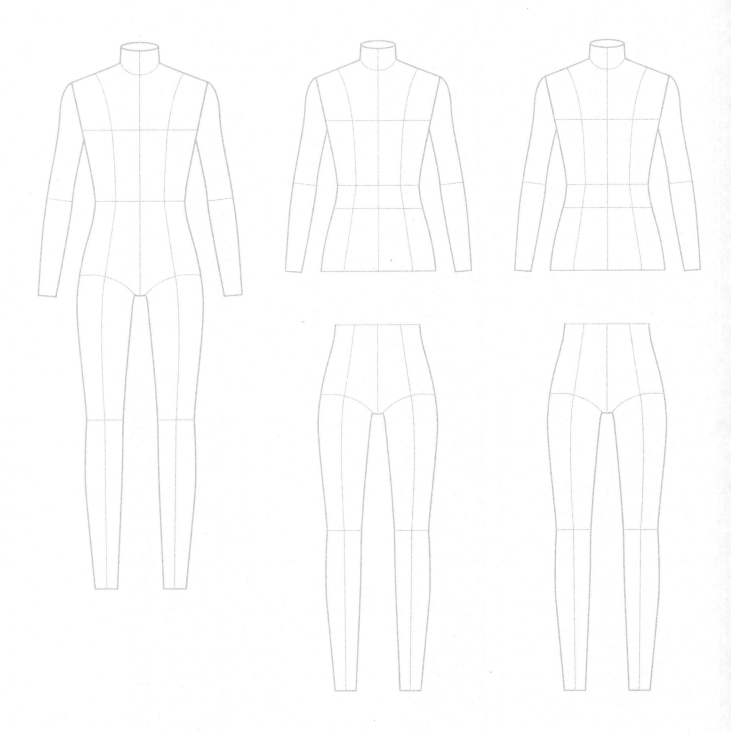

Note

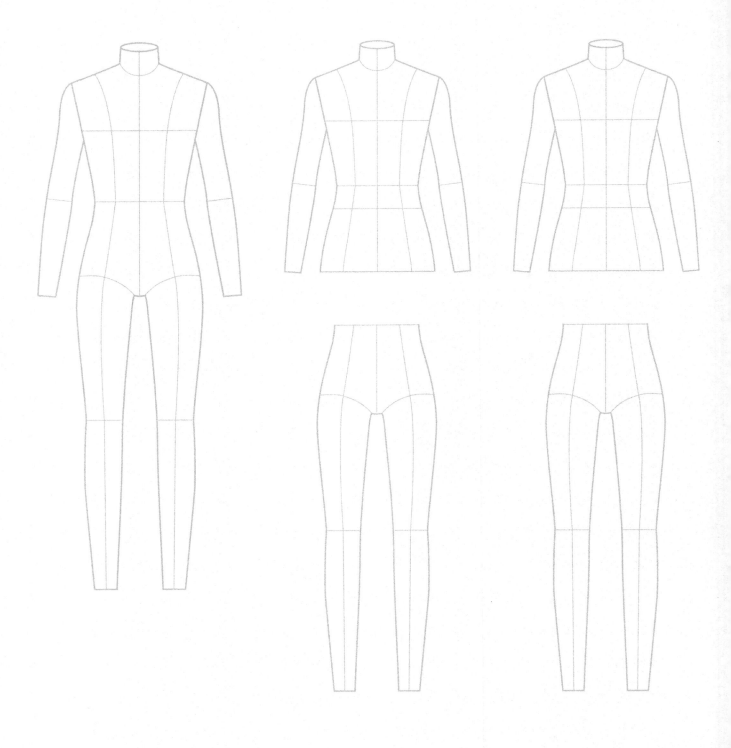

Note

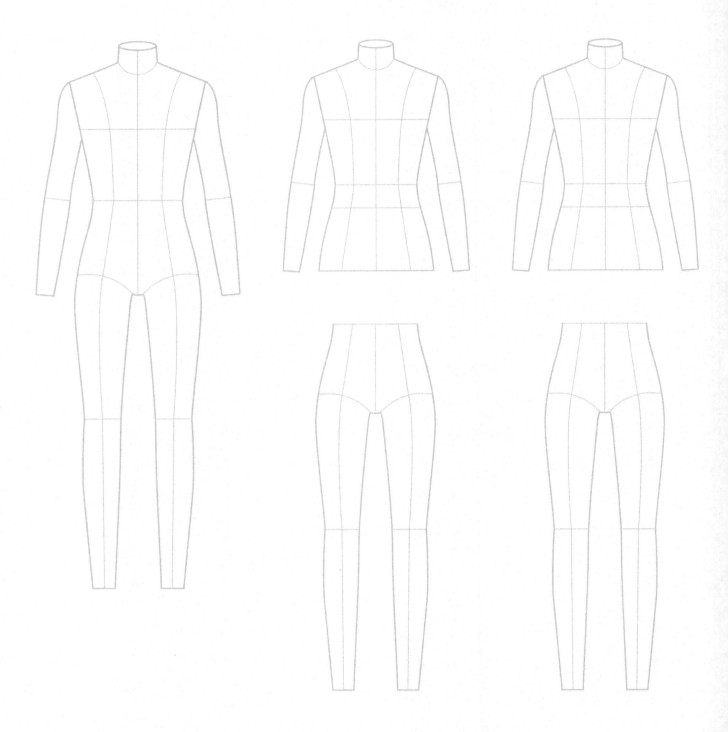

Note

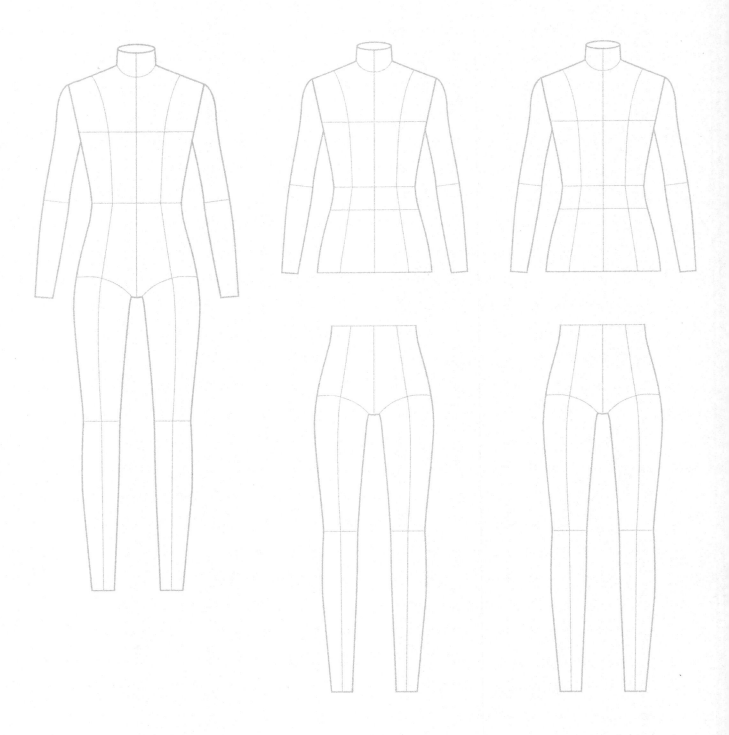

Note

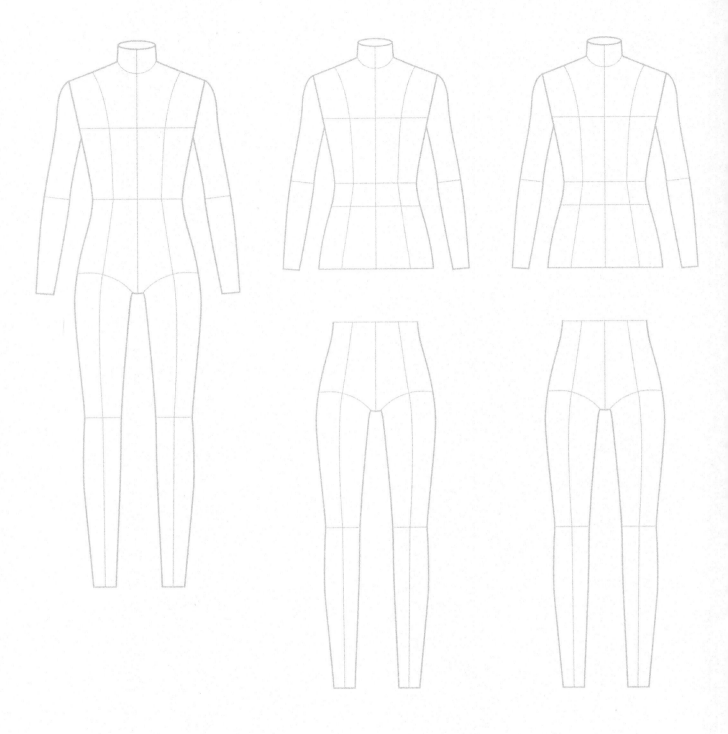

Note

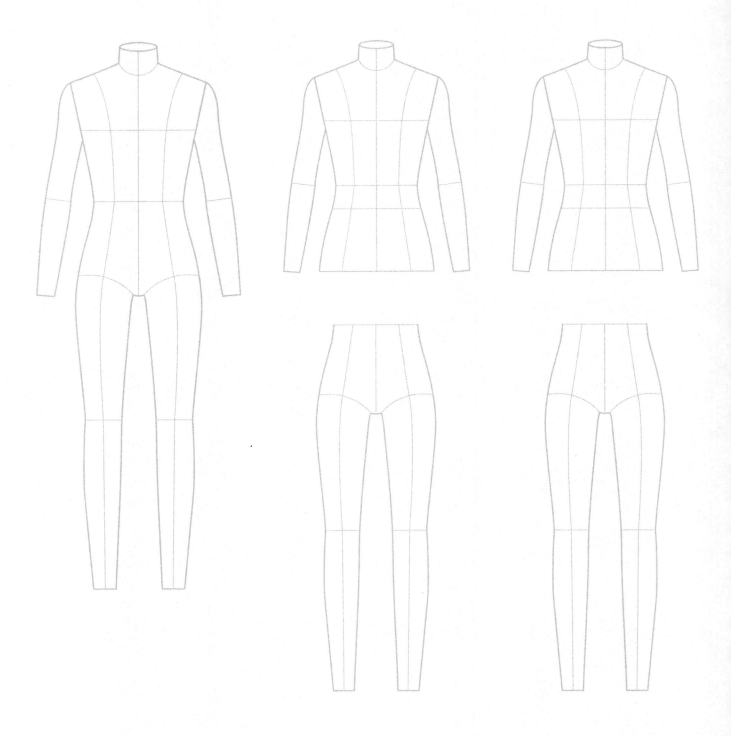

Note

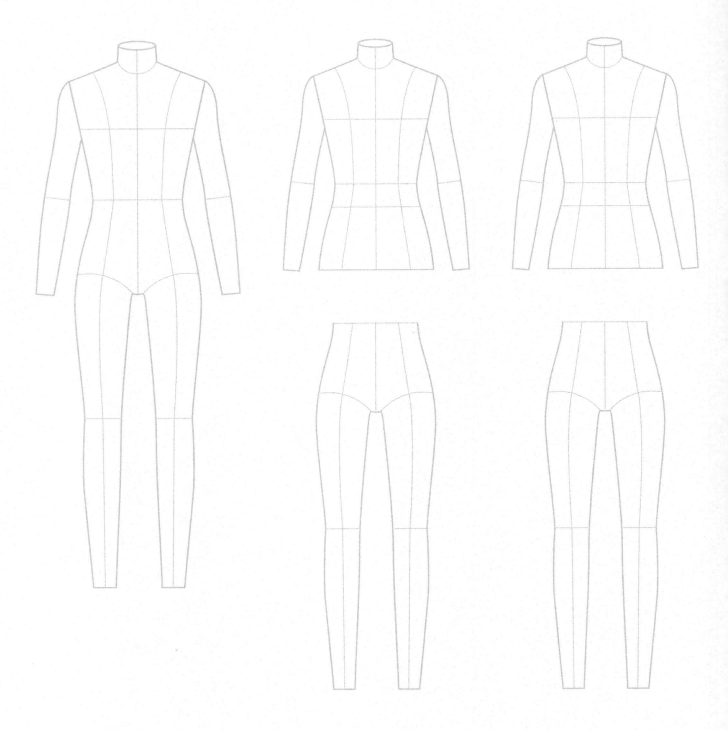

Note

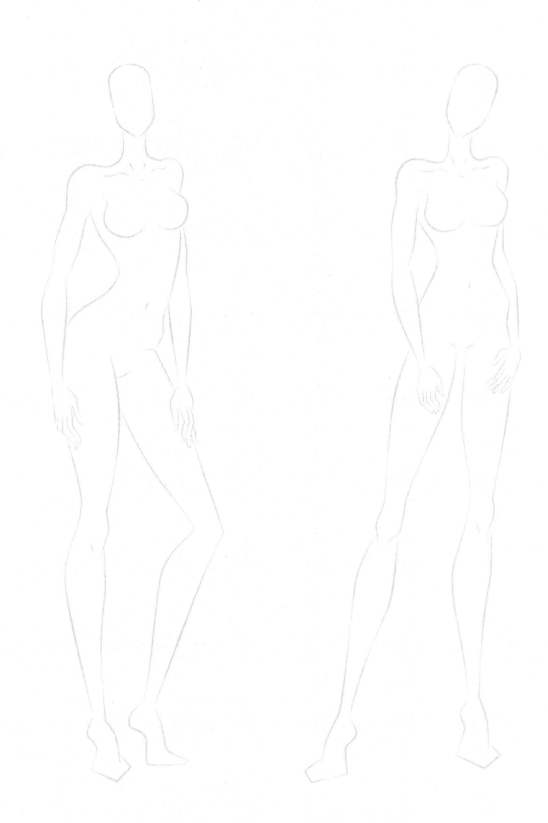

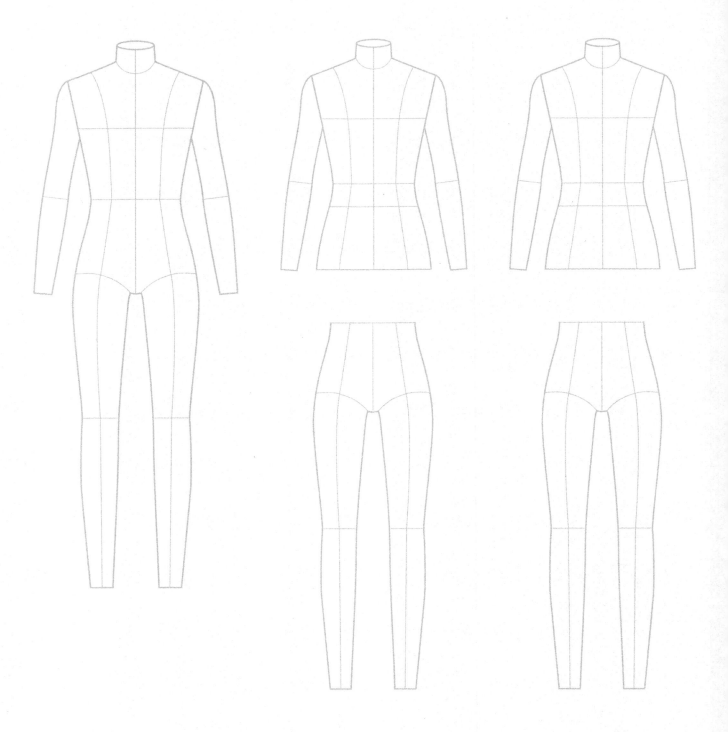

Note

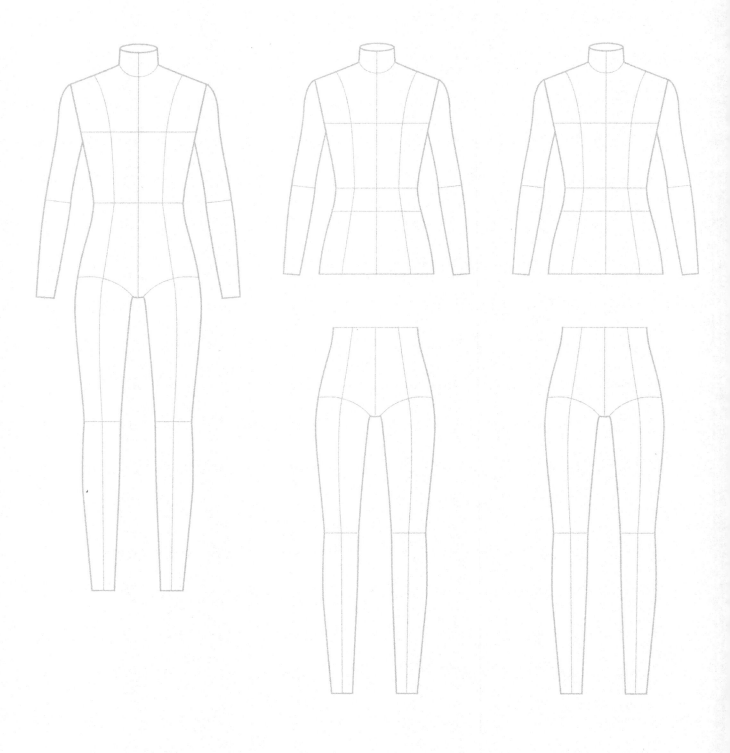

Note

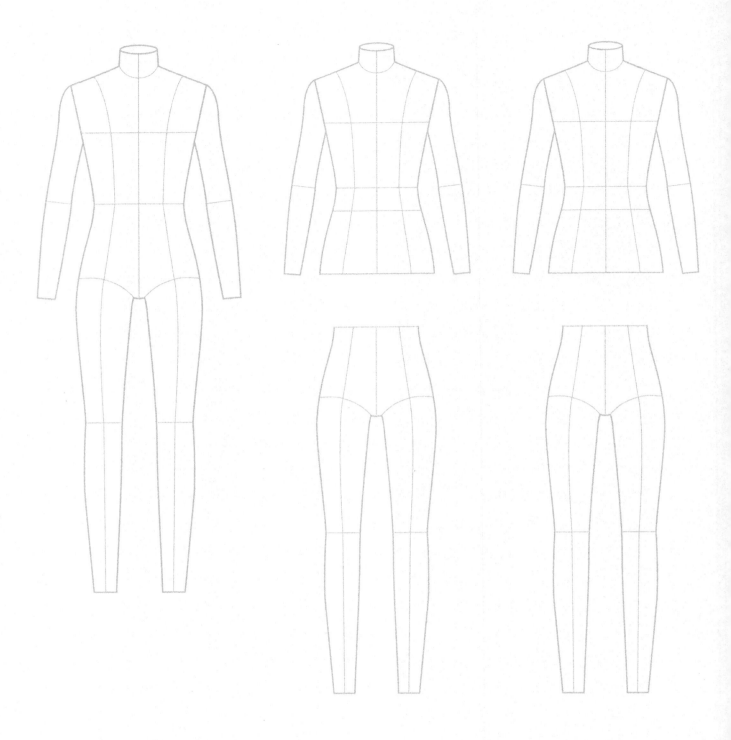

Note

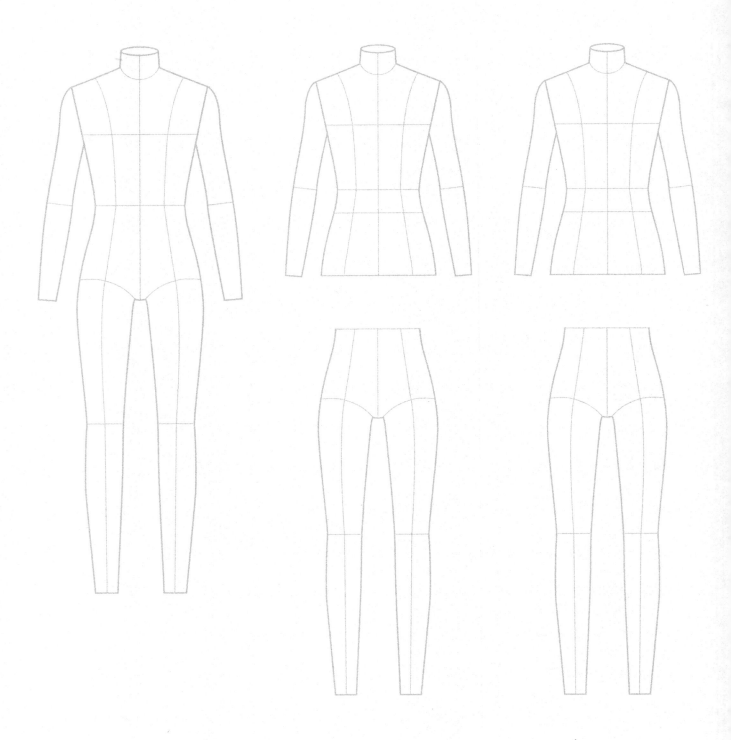

Note

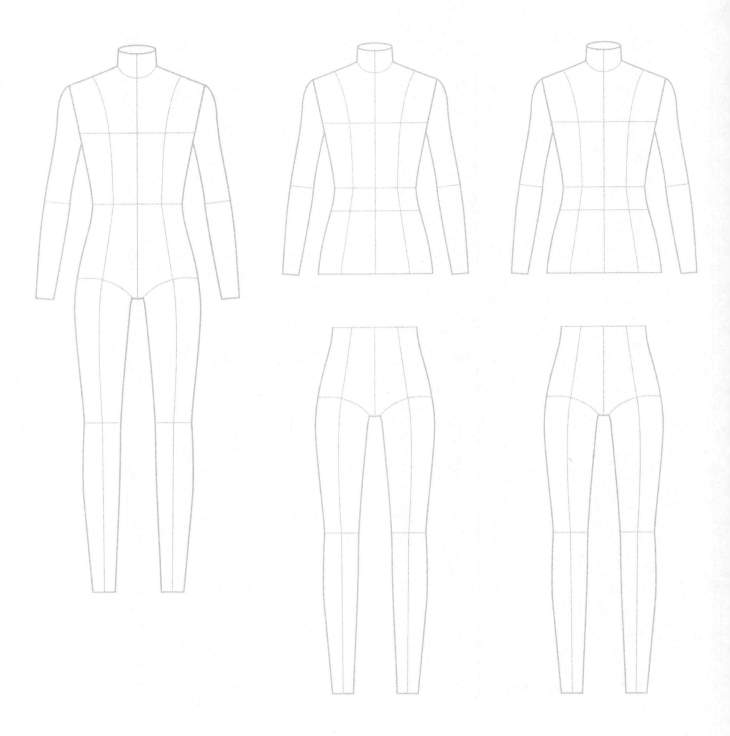

Note

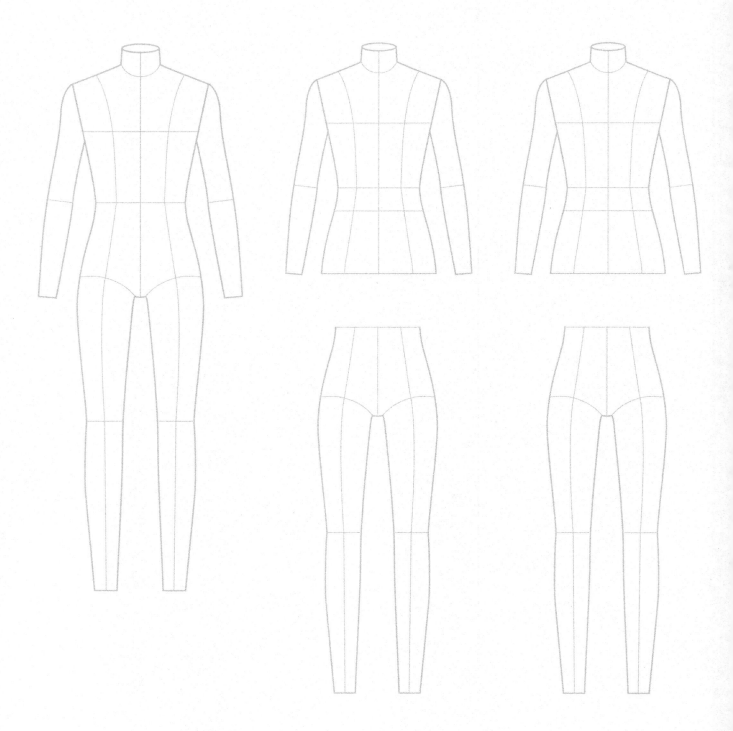

Note

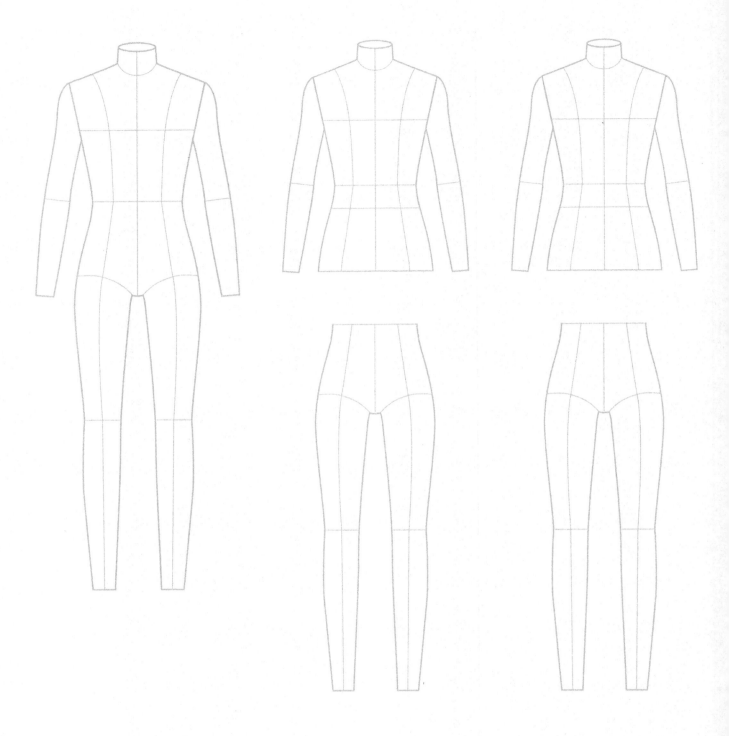

Note

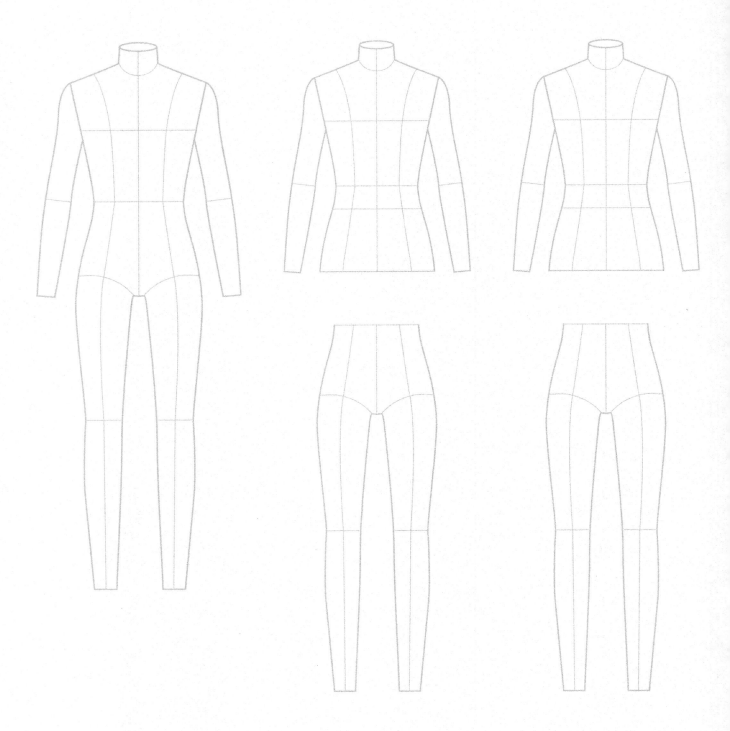

Note

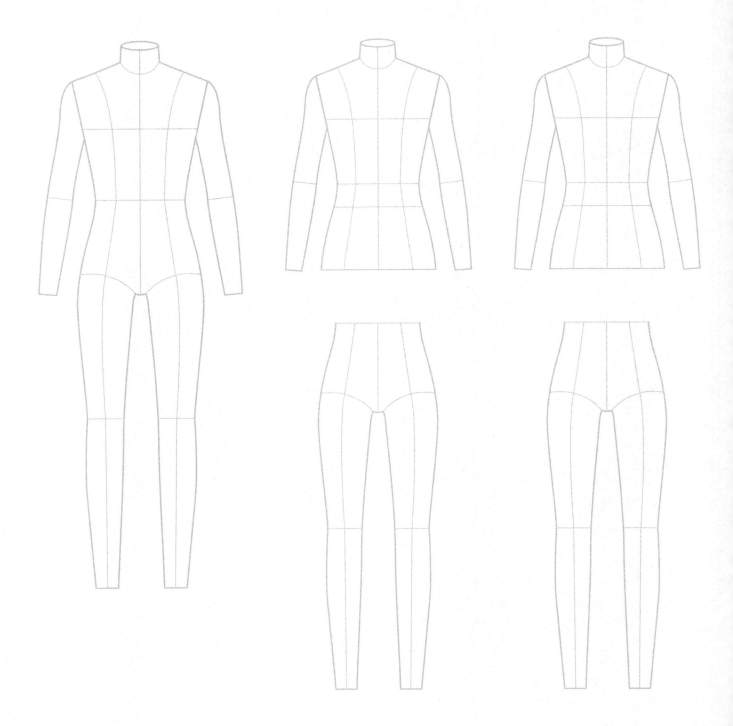

Note

Made in United States
North Haven, CT
26 June 2023

38264403R00063